I-SPY

BICYCLES

This book belongs to:

BMX

BMX stands for Bicycle Moto-cross. BMX bikes are not scaled down mountain bikes, they were invented in the mid 1970s, a few years before mountain bikes. They are small and agile, have 20-inch wheels and are used for short-course racing and trick riding.

I-Spy for ***5***

Downhill mountain bike

The earliest mountain bikes were only good downhill. Californian hippies took 1950s heavy 'clunker' bikes out onto the hills close to San Francisco and raced them downhill. To get them back to the top of the hill, riders either pushed them or hitched a ride in a truck. Subsequent development led to mountain bikes which could pedal uphill. Now there are specific downhill bikes which usually come fitted with front and rear suspension designed to soak up the knocks.

I-Spy for ***15***

Folding bike

Travelling with a bicycle isn't easy. They don't fit well into cars and many trains either charge cyclists extra money to carry their bicycles or refuse to carry them at all. Folding cycles are therefore excellent for getting around these restrictions. The best fold within 15-20 seconds.

*I-Spy for **15***

Freeriding fun bike

This is a mountain bike – often with front and rear suspension – which never gets anywhere near a mountain but is for posing on in urban areas or at race meetings. A sub-category of the fun bike is the 'cruiser', a bicycle based on the American utility bikes of the 1950s.

*I-Spy for **20***

Monocoque racing bike

Bicycle developers such as Mike Burrows like to experiment with different methods of making bicycles. Few people took carbon-fibre monocoque – i.e., 'one-piece' – frames seriously until Chris Boardman won an Olympic Gold medal on his Lotus Superbike.

*I-Spy for **20***

Mountain bike

Invented in the late 1970s, and radically improved in the 1980s, the mountain bike is now the most commonly-seen bicycle type in America, much of Europe and most of the rest of the world. It's only in China – home to the world's biggest population and greatest number of bicycles – that 'utility bikes' outnumber mountain bikes. Built to tackle off-road trails – mountain bikes are also known as ATBs, all-terrain bikes – most mountain bikes never get ridden on real mountains although their tough and chunky steel frames, powerful brakes and fat tyres could certainly manage it.

I-Spy for ***5***

◀ Recumbent

Famously banned from racing alongside 'normal' bicycles in 1934, recumbents are fast. Because the rider sits back and is closer to the ground he or she is more aerodynamically efficient. Average racers on recumbents built for speed can easily beat high-quality racing cyclists on traditional diamond-framed bicycles. Touring recumbents are also available but as the rider is sitting in a more upright 'deck-chair', much of the wind resistance gain is lost.

I-Spy for ***20***

Road racing bike ▶

A very lightweight, thin-tyred bicycle built for speed. The kind of bicycle – mostly built from steel tubes – used by riders in the Tour de France and other races.

I-Spy for ***10***

Tandem

A bicycle made for two. There are racing tandems, touring tandems and even mountain bike tandems. The 'captain' sits on the front and does all of the steering (and sometimes most of the pedalling!), while the 'stoker' sits on the back and cannot steer, although can sometimes brake independently of the captain. Visually impaired people can experience cycling by becoming stokers.

*I-Spy for **15***

Time trial bike

While road racing bikes are usually 'all rounders' – they can be used for sprinting, hill climbs, bunch riding and going fast – time trial bikes are built for speed only and often come in unusual shapes which help mould the cyclist into a 'tucked' aerodynamically efficient position.

*I-Spy for **15***

Touring bike

With padded, dropped handlebars, a tough diamond frame (almost always steel), aluminium racks for fitting pannier bags, and plenty of water bottle cages, touring bikes are built for long-distance travel. They have chunkier tyres than road racing bikes and can take a lot of battering. Mountain bikes can also be adapted to become touring bikes.
*I-Spy for **10***

Trekking bike

Also called 'hybrid' (because it's a combination between a road bike and a mountain bike) – or sports touring bike or utility bike – the trekking bike is an all-rounder, just as suitable for carrying shopping, riding to work or travelling around the world. The best come with mudguards, lights, and pannier racks.
*I-Spy for **10***

Trials bike

A cross between a BMX and a mountain bike. Trials bikes have fat tyres to soak up the knocks, very low gears and small frames. They are used exclusively for climbing over obstacles and pulling stunts. Sensible trials bike riders wear full protective clothing, including shin pads, gloves and a full-face helmet.

I-Spy for ***20***

Triathlon bike

This is very similar to a time trial bike. Triathlons are races that combine running, swimming and cycling. Since their introduction in the late 1970s, triathlons have been a breeding ground for innovations in cycling. The use of 'tri-bars', the handlebar extensions that get riders into extremely flat positions on their bikes, was popularised first in triathlons.

I-Spy for ***15***

Aston Martin

When famous British sports car maker Aston Martin wanted to produce an exclusive – and very expensive – mountain bike, they approached custom bike builder Chas Roberts of Croydon. He built a limited number of steel-framed Aston Martin bikes which were painted in the same colours as the cars.

I-Spy for ***100***

Audi

The Audi Quattro RV1pro has an aluminium 'Y' frame with front and rear suspension. Audi also produce a helmet and snazzy Lycra clothing to go with the bike.

I-Spy for ***25***

Birdy

Designed in Germany by Riesse and Mueller, built in Taiwan, the Birdy is a folding bike and has an aluminium frame equipped with front and rear suspension. Unlike other folding bikes which feel odd to ride, the riding position on the Birdy was designed to mimic that found on comfortable road bikes.

I-Spy for ***25***

British Eagle

Known for their excellent touring and mountain bikes, British Eagle's steel-framed Cambridge is a new departure for the Lancashire company. It is a futuristic utility bike, and comes with a Shimano 7-speed hub gear, a front basket, a rear rack, mudguards and a bell.

I-Spy for ***20***

The 'Brompton '

This is a folding bicycle invented by British designer Andrew Ritchie. The frame splits in two places. An elastomer spring, where the frame meets the back wheel, acts as suspension. The basic model comes without front or rear racks, dynamo lights or the folding pedal option.

I-Spy for ***15***

Budget Bootbike

Budget Rent-a-Car are a worldwide car rental agency with 154 branches in the UK. The latest addition to their fleet is the Bootbike, a steel framed mountain bike with hinges on the centre of the frame allowing the bike to fold. Whilst not suitable for train travel – standard folding bikes have small wheels too – the Bootbike is perfect for putting in car boots.

I-Spy for ***15***

Cannondale

In the 1980s Cannondale were famous for producing extremely fat-tubed aluminium bicycles. The Raven Super V, however, is very different to 'normal' Cannondale bikes. It features thermoplastic tubes formed into a 'Y' frame, and has suspension front and rear.

I-Spy for ***25***

Claud Butler

Claud Butler is a long-established and prestigioius British bicycle company. This is a steel-framed Claud Butler Pagan mountain bike although the company is most famous for its Claud Butler Majestic touring bikes.
*I-Spy for **5***

Condor

Condor Cycles is a London bike shop established in 1945 which specialises in road racing bikes. Their Italia Veloce has a handbuilt Reynolds 531 frame and an Italian Campagnolo gear groupset making it a traditionally-styled racing bike for purists.
*I-Spy for **15***

Daewoo

The Korean car manufacturer now has a bicycle range. Ari Hadijipetrou, one of the people responsible for introducing Muddy Fox into the UK, helped them develop their bicycles. This is the CTB – a steel-framed city bike with Nexus internal hub gears.
*I-Spy for **20***

Dawes

Dawes, although a long-established and well-known British company, is actually owned by a Dutch group who own a number of European bicycle brands. The Dutch influence is clear in the Street Vision which looks very much like the 'Roadsters' common in Holland. It is equipped with a 7-speed Shimano Nexus hub. Dawes also produce touring bikes, a folder, commuting bikes, mountain bikes and a recumbent.

I-Spy for ***10***

De Kerf

The Canadian-built De Kerf Generation race bike has a steel frame kitted out with Rock Shox Judy C suspension forks. De Kerf bikes are rare in Europe, and used mainly for serious mountain bike racing.

I-Spy for ***25***

Emmelle
When British cycle accessories company Moore Large wanted to produce a bike range they called it Emmelle (i.e., ML). Made in the Far East, Emmelle bikes are budget machines. The saddle has a built-in LED safety light which is operated when the brakes are squeezed.
I-Spy for ***5***

Falcon
Long-established British manufacturer Falcon of Lincolnshire makes budget and mid-priced bikes. The Mag Race 3 has a steel frame and oversized forks. It's powered by Shimano 21 speed TY 22 gears and has Gripshift gear shifters. The five-spoked wheels are made by Vuelta of Italy.
I-Spy for ***15***

Giant
Giant is the second largest bicycle manufacturer in Taiwan.As well as budget models, Giant also produce top-of-the-range bikes such as the TCR 1 Pro seen here. Designed by Mike Burrows, the TCR series of road racing bikes are unique in that one frame size suits (almost) all. To find the perfect fit, riders make modifications to the handlebar stem and seat post .
*I-Spy for **20***

GT
American bicycle company GT is best known for its mountain bikes and its mountain bike team, but it started life as a maker of BMXs. This aluminium framed GT is similar to one ridden by GT team member Hans Rey, the world's top bicycle stunt rider. Hans 'No Way' Rey tours the world giving demonstrations of his breathtaking riding skills.
*I-Spy for **10***

Kawasaki
Much more famous for their motorbikes, Kawasaki produce a small range of steel-framed bicycles, including this, the K-MB 450. The Kawasaki mountain bike racing team was once a common sight at UK races but has now been disbanded. Kawasaki bikes are now very rarely seen.
*I-Spy for **25***

KHE
KHE are a German BMX company, producing expensive freestyle and racing BMXs. The Beater has a steel frame and comes with peg bosses on the front wheel for standing on and pulling stunts.
*I-Spy for **15***

Kingcycle

Designed by Miles Kingsbury of Buckinghamshire the Kingcycle is a short-wheelbase recumbent. The frame and forks are made from Reynolds 531 steel tubes. Kingcycles are always yellow. The plastic box on the back fairing contains LED lights and has a hinged lid: it has enough storage space to take a lock, a packed lunch, and a waterproof jacket.
I-Spy for ***20***

Kona

Canadian mountain bike company Kona produce a range of bicycles, named after volcanic features of Hawaii. The Hei Hei is a top-of-the range aluminium framed racing mountain bike, equipped with Marzocchi Bomber suspension forks and a Shimano XTR groupset.
I-Spy for ***25***

Land Rover

British-company Pashley produce modified Moulton space-framed bicycles for Land Rover. The separable triangulated 'space frame' on this, the APB (All Purpose Bicycle), has leading link front suspension, bonded rubber rear suspension and 20 inch wheels.

I-Spy for ***20***

Marin ▸

American bike company Marin is named after Marin County California which is where mountain biking was invented. The Marin Rift Zone has an aluminium frame and Manitou Mach 5 Pro C suspension forks. A feature too small to notice on the Marin bikes available in the UK is the fitting of a 'Datatag', a transponder the size of a grain of rice. This can be read by a 'tagging gun' issued to the police and means Marin bikes can easily be reunited with their owners should they be stolen and then recovered.

I-Spy for ***15***

◂ Mercedes-Benz

With its matt aluminium frame, this bike from the famous German car manufacturer is hard to miss. Among its unique features is the belt-driven drivetrain: with no oily chain there are no more snagged and dirty trousers, but the belt system is not as efficient as a chain-driven set-up.

I-Spy for ***100***

Moulton

Dr. Alex Moulton, designer of the Moulton bicycle, developed the suspension for the very first Mini motorcar. He brought his skills to cycling and in 1962 launched a small-wheeled bicycle with suspension front and rear. Small wheels mean greater acceleration.
I-Spy for ***15***

Muddy Fox

Now owned by an Indian company, Muddy Fox started life in the fertile imaginations of Ari Hadjipetrou and Drew Fox, who were responsible for popularising the mountain bike in Britain. Muddy Fox wasn't the first mountain bike available in the UK but it was easily the most well known.
I-Spy for ***20***

Orange

Orange bikes are built in Taiwan to a high specification. The steel-framed P7 is a confirmed favourite with dedicated mountain bike racers looking for a mid-priced machine. The P7, like other Orange bikes, has no standard specification; owners can mix and match components before they buy.
I-Spy for ***10***

Orbit
Built in Dudley in the West Midlands, the Orbit Discovery is a steel-framed trekking bike suitable for shopping, commuting and short tours. There are two versions: one has 7-speed Sachs gears and the other has a 21-speed derailleur set-up. Orbit also produce recumbent bicycles.
I-Spy for ***10***

Pashley
Best known for producing traditional English bicycles more in keeping with the 1950s than the 1990s, Pashley also produce work bicycles such as butcher's bikes and postman's bikes. A recent addition to their stable of exotic bicycles is the Tube Rider, inspired by American cruiser bicycles and British BSA bicycles of the 1950s, although as it comes with Sturmey Archer 5-speed hub gears and a sprung Brooks B66 leather saddle the Tube Rider is a practical bicycle, not just a posing machine.
I-Spy for ***10***

Peugeot ▸
Peugeot may be best known for making cars but it started life in 1887 as a manufacturer of steel hoops for women's dresses! The company soon diversified into making bicycles and, later, cars. It is the biggest bike builder in France, making everything from cheap and heavy street bikes to state-of-the-art racers. The Richard Virenque model lies in the middle: it has a steel frame and is named after a famous hill-climbing racing cyclist.
*I-Spy for **10***

Porsche ▾
Porsche, the German sports car manufacturer, recently joined forces with Votec, a German cycle company, to produce the Porsche-S front suspension mountain bike. The gears are by Sachs and the hydraulic brakes by Magura. And, just like the cars, if you need to ask the price you can't afford the bike!
*I-Spy for **100***

Pro•Flex

Girven Pro-Flex is an American bicycle brand. Its first product was a suspension handlebar stem which got its 'bounce' from an elastomer wedge. The company expanded and starting producing full suspension bicycles. All Pro-Flex bicycles – they only make mountain bikes – have front and rear elastomer suspension. The Pro-Flex 955 has an aluminium frame.
*I-Spy for **15***

Raleigh

Started in Nottingham in 1895 (the name comes from the first premises, in Raleigh Street) the company grew rapidly and, thanks to the genius of the first chairman, Frank Bowden, started to sponsor well-known cycle racers. The Raleigh name spread worldwide. Today Raleigh produce 600 000 bicycles a year, many for export. The Monsoon is a steel girls' bike equipped with 18 Shimano gears with GripShift handlebar shifters.
*I-Spy for **5***

Real

Halfords' superstores sell over 40 percent of all the new bikes in the UK. Real is their latest own-brand range and consists of a hybrid (the Cafe – pictured here); a cruiser (the Easy); a touring bike (the Eco) and an aluminium mountain bike (the Pure). The Cafe has a fully-enclosed 4-speed Nexus internal hub gear.

*I-Spy for **10***

Ribble

Handbuilt in England, Ribble bicycles are made by a cycle shop in Lancashire. The shop specialises in competition road racing cycles. This particular Ribble cycle is made from steel and is equipped with Shimano Dura-ace gears.

*I-Spy for **20***

Schwinn

Schwinn cruisers were the favourite bikes of American paper boys in the 1950s. Although heavy and cumbersome the cruiser later went on to inspire the invention of the mountain bike and is now available in the original form for use as a 'posing' bike. The original Cruisers were modelled on motorbikes and some even had fake petrol tanks. Modern versions, such as this one – the Schwinn Cruiser Deluxe – are equipped with Shimano Nexus hub gears.

*I-Spy for **15***

Scott

This North American company produces ski accessories as well as bikes. Their top-of-the-range models – such as this Elite Racing bike – have 'Endorphin' frames made from thermoplastics, a form of carbon fibre.

*I-Spy for **20***

Specialized
When mountain bikes were first invented they were either custom-built or modified versions of old 'cruiser' frames. The first company to produce a commercial mountain bike was America's Specialized. Their Rockhopper bike was responsible for much of the later success of mountain biking. Each year the company bring out a new Rockhopper and one version, the A1 FS, is now equipped with front suspension – Rockshox Indy C forks – as standard. The first Rockhopper was steel, the latest one is aluminium although a steel version is also available.
*I-Spy for **10***

Trek
Designed in America, built in Taiwan, Trek is one of the world's leading bicycle brands. The frame of the Trek 7000 is made from high-grade Easton EA60 ProGram tapered aluminium fitted with Rockshox Indy C suspension forks.
*I-Spy for **10***

Universal Cycles

This chromed 'freestyle' BMX – the Hammerhead – has a steel frame with 20 inch wheels and 'pegs' on the front wheel. Riders stand on these to pull stunts and tricks. Universal bikes are made in Poland.
*I-Spy for **5***

Windcheetah

Designed by Mike Burrows (see Giant), the Windcheetah is made under licence by the Cheshire-based Seat of the Pants Company. It's a very low-to-the-ground, trike recumbent and has a terrific turn of speed: it can reach 70mph on a long downhill stretch. The frame is made from aluminium; the seat from carbon kevlar. A full fairing – a carbon fibre cover – can be fitted to the Windcheetah to reduce drag even further.
*I-Spy for **25***

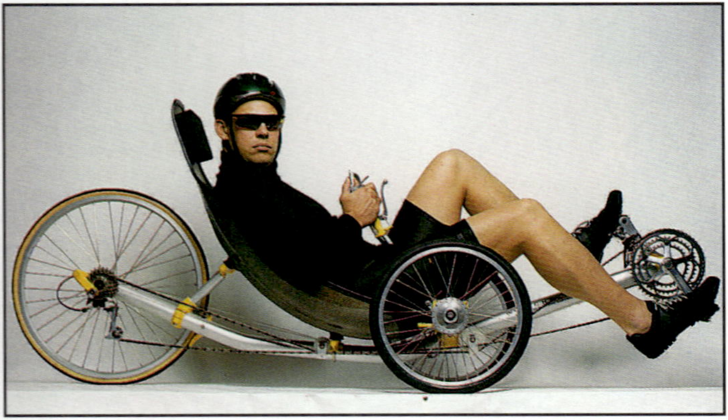

Hobby horses
The idea of balancing on two wheels did not occur to anybody until 1817 when Baron von Drais of Germany patented his wooden Laufmaschine, or 'running machine'. The English gentry were soon riding iron 'Hobby Horses' with steering. This picture shows gentlemen being taught at Johnson's riding school in London.
*I-Spy for **100***

Velocipede
Between 1839 and 1842 the Scottish blacksmith, Kirkpatrick Macmillan, made the next radical step in bicycle design by providing a Hobby Horse with continuous drive to the back wheel via pedals. This was the first true bicycle although it was not widely seen outside Scotland. In the 1860s, Pierre Michaux, a Parisian manufacturer of invalid carriages, added pedals to the front wheel of a Hobby Horse and this evolved into the velocipede pictured here.
*I-Spy for **30***

Penny Farthing

Because the velocipede was directly driven from the front wheel the only way to cover more ground with each pedal revolution was to increase the size of the wheel. This led to the creation of Ordinary bicycles, also known as Penny Farthings (so called because they resembled coins of the time).

*I-Spy for **25***

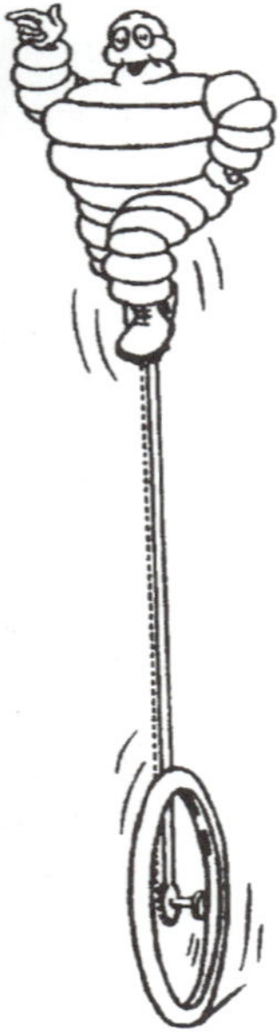

Safety bicycle

With riders on Penny Farthings being so high, riding one was a dangerous activity. Later, improved bicycles, very similar to modern bikes, were called Safety cycles. This is an early example. Note there are still no pneumatic tyres so the ride was very hard.

*I-Spy for **25***

The Chopper

An American idea imported into Britain in 1970 by Raleigh, the Chopper bicycle was meant to look like a motorbike, the kind of laid-back machine made famous by the film *Easy Rider*. Despite being rather impractical it was hugely successful, selling 750 000 units in ten years.
*I-Spy for **20***

Cruiser

Popular with American paper boys, Schwinn cruisers were designed to look similar to motorbikes and were consequently very heavy. Their main claim to fame now is that they went on to inspire the invention of mountain bikes in the 1980s.
*I-Spy for **15***

The Future

Cycle component manufacturer, Shimano, sponsors the annual Bicycle Design competition to find the cycle designs of the future. Some of the designs will never be commercially viable, but others from previous years are starting to appear in bike shops. The selection pictured here are the winners from the design contest held in 1997.

*I-Spy for **50** any one bike entered for the competition*

The Zike

Sir Clive Sinclair was responsible for many of the brilliant consumer electronic inventions of the past twenty years: the digital watch, the home computer and the calculator were all his developments. His battery-powered Zike was not so successful, coming so soon after the demise of the C5, a battery powered recumbent bicycle.

*I-Spy for **30***

Butcher's or grocer's bike

The Delibike by Pashley of Stratford-upon-Avon is used by butchers and greengrocers. Goods for delivery are placed in the wicker basket on the front of the bike.
*I-Spy for **10***

Cycle Courier

With city streets blocked with traffic, often the quickest way to deliver a package is by using a cycle courier. They are well known for 'stretching the rules' as here on the streets of Dublin, mixing it with pedestrians.
*I-Spy for **10***

Goods delivery courier

For bulky deliveries some city courier firms use 'pedicabs'. These are specially-built recumbents and can either have a storage compartment fitted or space for carrying people.
*I-Spy for **25***

Newspaper deliveries
A common sight during the morning and early evening, paper boys and girls often use their bikes to get around quickly and efficiently.
I-Spy for ***5***

Policeman ▶
A policeman on a bike used to be an everyday sight but with the rising popularity of cars since the 1950s fewer and fewer bobbies patrolled their beat on a bicycle. This is slowly changing and many British police forces are now equipping some of their officers with high-tech mountain bikes. Bicycles are often quicker through town and police men and women on bikes can creep up on criminals silently. American cities such as Seattle introduced police cyclists ten years ago and have seen an improvement in their crime clear-up statistics.
I-Spy for ***20***

Postman ◀
Pashley Cycles of Stratford-upon-Avon have recently supplied thousands of specially built 'postman bikes' to the Post Office. A postman on a bike is a common sight throughout the British Isles.
I-Spy for ***10***

Professional mountain biker

With no help allowed from fellow team members or spectators, a professional mountain bike racer is entirely self-reliant. Unlike road racing cyclists, mountain bike racers have to carry all their own spares during a race. Each rider races for him or herself: there are no team tactics as in races such as the Tour de France.
*I-Spy for **15***

Professional road racing cyclist

Winning a stage of the world famous Tour de France is the dream of every professional racing cyclist.
*I-Spy for **20** any road race, double for the Tour de France*

Professional trials rider

Trials riders don't have to be especially fit but the activity is too dangerous for anybody without a great deal of natural talent to do safely. Trials riders travel the world showing off their skills and are often seen at trade shows and as warm-up events at mountain bike races.

I-Spy for ***20***

Rickshaw pilot

Tourists in cities such as York and Oxford can hitch a ride from the same kind of rickshaw taxis used in the Far East. Normally such services are only available in the summer months. Rickshaw taxis need special licences.

I-Spy for ***25***

Tour guide

It's difficult for cars to get around many towns and cities with medieval centres and so walking and cycling tours are popular with tourists. This group of American tourists are being guided around the centre of York.

I-Spy for ***20***

Helmets

When you fall off a bike, nine times out of ten you'll not touch your head on the ground. But that tenth time could seriously hurt you and can even lead to brain damage. That's why helmets are so important. They protect you from low-speed crashes onto rocks, against tree branches and onto kerb stones: they do not protect you from injury should you be hit by a car. Cycling safely is the only way to avoid injury.

*I-Spy for **5***

Body armour

Downhill mountain bikers can injury themselves if they fall off their bikes at speed. Lightweight body armour can help minimise injuries.

*I-Spy for **10***

Advanced stop-line
Many local authorities have installed advanced stop-lines at busy junctions. Cyclists go to the head of the queue and can start off before cars which is necessary to stop cars 'cutting' in front of them. Unfortunately the Land Rover driver in this picture obviously doesn't know the rules!
I-Spy for ***10***

Traffic lights
Many cycle safety measures are appearing in our towns and cities. As well as the 'green man' on pedestrian crossings there are now some traffic lights which feature the 'green bicycle'.
I-Spy for ***15***

Sam Browne belt

The fluorescent yellow strips that link together across the shoulder and on the stomach are called Sam Browne belts. The bright yellow is highly visible during the day and the sash is also reflective making cyclists visible to car drivers at night too.

I-Spy for ***5***

Front lamp

Cycle lights are never as bright as car headlamps. Cyclists don't use their lights to see the road ahead, they use them to be seen by motorists and pedestrians. The Ever Ready illuminator is fitted with a halogen bulb, and is very bright.

I-Spy for ***5***

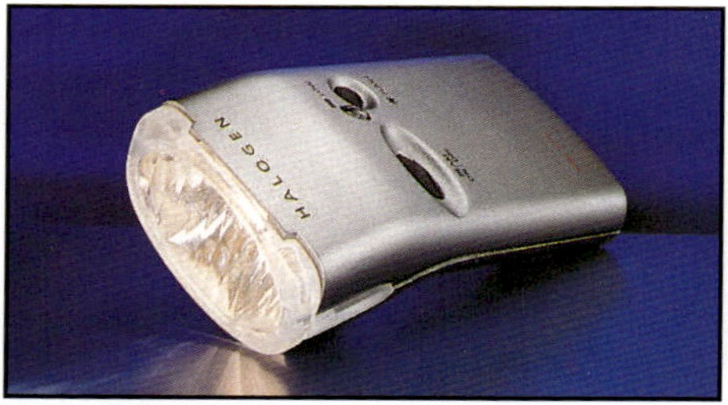

Reflec ink

A Manchester company has developed an ink that when printed onto garments acts like a covering of millions of microscopic cats' eyes. Made from tiny metallised glass beads, Reflec ink can be printed onto almost anything. It can be made in any colour and only flares up when light is shone upon it. Unlike 'retro-reflective' strips, which don't light up the body shape of the wearer, Reflec makes it easier for motorists to see what is up ahead.

I-Spy for ***10***

Segregated paths

To make sure cyclists and fast-moving motorised traffic meet as infrequently as possible, many local authorities are creating cycle paths. Pedestrians walk on one side; cyclists ride along the other.

*I-Spy for **10***

LED light

Used in flashing mode a rear LED light is very effective at night, and much more noticeable than a more powerful, but static, red light. LED stands for Light Emitting Diode and uses very little energy: batteries can therefore last for many weeks, making LED lights very popular with cyclists.

*I-Spy for **5***

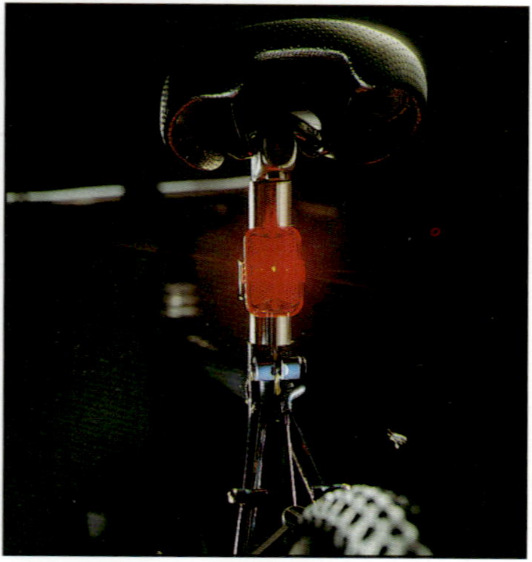

The Goodies Bike ▲

Made famous in the 1970s by the comedy trio, the Goodies, their three-person bicycle – a trandem – was originally built in the 1930s as a tandem. A third seat was added in the 1970s. The bike weighs 35kgs and is 10ft long. In 1990 three crazy cyclists crossed Africa riding it!
*I-Spy for **30***

◀ The Buddy-Bike

Riders should be approximately the same weight to ride on the Buddybike, for obvious reasons. Riders share braking and pedalling but, naturally, only one person can steer.
*I-Spy for **25**.*

Freightmate

The Pashley Freight-mate is a weight-carrying trike and can haul heavy and bulky items with comparative ease.
*I-Spy for **30**.*

The Muni

Another Pashley product, the Muni is a Mountain Unicycle. Some riders use Munis on events like the Polaris Challenge, a two-day mountain bike orienteering event. Needless to say they never win but they never come last either.
*I-Spy for **20**.*

Peer Gynt

The Peer Gynt is a long wheelbase recumbent. It is a German touring recumbent and has a 'deck chair' seat. A trike version is also available.
*I-Spy for **25***

Velocita

The Velocita, despite its Italian sounding name, is a British-built short wheelbase recumbent. It's made from aluminium, and the steering column is underneath the seat.
*I-Spy for **30***

Panniers

Cycle tourists and commuters store things in pannier bags which fit onto aluminium pannier racks.

I-Spy for ***5***

Carrying kids

For when children are too young to cycle by themselves a child trailer can ferry them about in comfort. This is the top-of-the-range Burley trailer from America.

I-Spy for ***15.***

Carrying a bike on a car
The tandem rack from Pendle Engineering of Lancashire, secures a tandem to a car's roof rack. Other racks are available which attach solo bikes to towball mounts or to the back windscreens of hatchback cars.
I-Spy for ***20.***

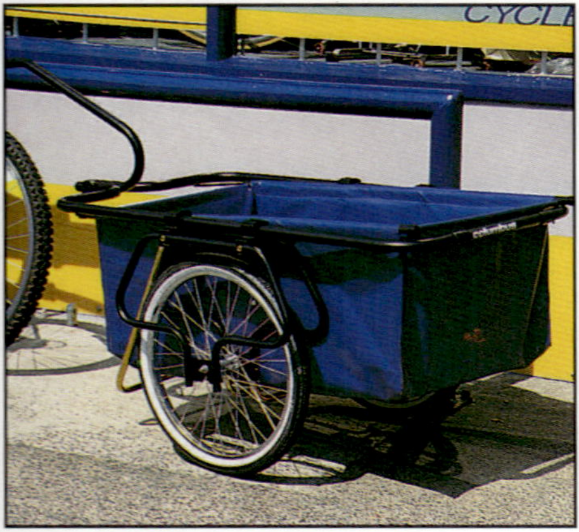

Carrying heavy loads
The Colombus trailer from America has a lightweight aluminium frame which can fold down for storage. It attaches to the seat post by a trailing arm.
I-Spy for ***25***.

Cycle shorts ▶

With padded inserts and thigh-hugging long legs, Lycra cycle shorts make cycling more comfortable than it otherwise would be.

I-Spy for ***5***

◀ Cycle jersey

Made from materials which 'wick' sweat away from the body and don't flap in the wind, skin-tight cycle jerseys are worn by serious cyclists.

I-Spy for ***10.***

Windproof jacket

Most windproof jackets designed for cycling – and other outdoor pursuits – are made from Pertex, a tightly-woven nylon material manufactured in Lancashire. The 'windchill' factor can make cyclists cold: even just a very thin windproof jacket can prevent this.

I-Spy for ***5***

Waterproof jacket

Most days a cyclist can get by with just a windproof jacket because even when it's raining a Pertex jacket will dry out rapidly. On those days when it rains non-stop some form of greater protection is needed. This Gore-Tex jacket from Manchester company Sprayway is waterproof and 'breathable', meaning water can't get in but water droplets (i.e., perspiration) can get out.
*I-Spy for **5***

SPD pedals

Racing cyclists used to have toe-clips to keep their feet attached to the pedals. Now they use binding systems developed to keep ski-boots attached to skis: the SPD system (Shimano Pedalling Dynamics).
*I-Spy for **10**.*

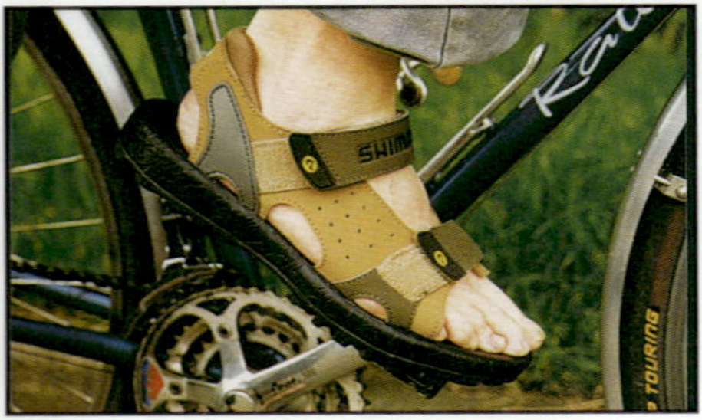

SPD sandals

Being linked to the bike improves pedalling efficiency. As well as special shoes fitted with SPD 'cleats', Shimano also produce SPD sandals, perfect for the summer.
*I-Spy for **20**.*

Michelin Wildgripper
The Wildgripper mountain bike tyre comes in six versions: professional racing, standard racing, muddy course racing, pinch resistant, rock riding and city riding.
I-Spy for ***10***

Garmin-GPS II
This Global Positioning System uses satellites to track your exact position. It continuously scans data from up to 8 satellites for fast and accurate positioning wherever you are in the world.
I-Spy for ***25***

Middleburn crankset

All bikes come equipped with front chainwheels (on mountain bikes there are normally three chainwheels; road bikes have two) but many cyclists upgrade. Middleburn produce chainsets and other drivetrain components in jazzy colours. Most commercial chainwheels are 'pressed' out of sheet aluminium; the Middleburn ones are CNC machined for extra strength.
*I-Spy for **20***

Nexus hubs

Nexus by Shimano offers lightweight, easy to ride, multiple gear bikes without the complexity of derailleurs and external calliper or cantilever brakes. The derailleur is eliminated by an internally geared rear hub.
*I-Spy for **15***

Pace suspension fork ▶

The RC-36 Pro-Class MXCD is a lightweight suspension fork with 76mm of travel. It uses coil springs and a hydraulic cartridge.

I-Spy for ***15***

Sigma Sport cycle computer ▼

This small electronic measuring device provides information on speed, cadence (pedal revolutions per minute), trip distance travelled, total distance travelled and other functions.

I-Spy for ***10***

◀ Shimano STX-RC groupset

This selection of equipment includes the RD-MC38 Rear Derailleur which is of 8 speed advance light action design as well as having long-wearing chromized steel pulley bushings. The FH-R080-S Freehub has a roller clutch freewheel mechanism for silent freewheeling. It also has an aluminium alloy quick release.

I-Spy for ***15***

Urathon solid tyres
Made from a polymer sponge material to act like a tyre and inner tube, the Urathon 'solid' tyre can be ridden over a bed of nails but will never puncture.
*I-Spy for **15***

◄ Titec saddle
Most saddles are covered in leather which cycle shorts can easily slip on. To prevent this slipping, some saddle manufacturers offer saddles embroidered with logos.
*I-Spy for **15***

V-Brake ►
The Shimano V-Brake offers awesome stopping power. The V-Brake has longer arms than normal cantilever brakes and can deliver more braking power with less effort at the lever.
*I-Spy for **5***

Bruce Bursford

He couldn't do it on the road – too much rolling resistance – but on rollers Bruce Bursford recently reached a world record speed of 207.9mph. His Lola composite bike has a front chainwheel with an amazing 126-teeth! A front chainwheel normally has only 52 teeth.
*I-Spy for **50.***

Andy Wilkinson

Endurance rider, Andy Wilkinson, broke the End-to-End speed record in April 1996. He cycled from Lands End to John O'Groats in just 41 hours, shaving 4 hours off the previous record set by … Andy Wilkinson. His previous record was set on a conventional road racing bike, his latest one was set in this faired Windcheetah.
*I-Spy for **50**.*

ISBN 1 85671 183 8
Michelin Tyre Public Limited Company
Edward Hyde Building, 38 Clarendon Road, Watford, Herts, WD1 1SX
MICHELIN and the Michelin Man are Registered Trademarks of Michelin

Compiled by Carlton Reid; Designed by Grahame Dudley Associates.

The publisher gratefully acknowledges the contribution of Front Page Creations and Carlton Reid who provided the majority of the photographs in this book, also Jim McGurn/Open Road and G. Steve Cory for their copyright photographs.
A CIP record for this title is available from the British Library.

Colour reproduction by Anglia Colour. Printed by Graficromo SA, Spain.